MADDER

Also by David Constantine

A Brightness to Cast Shadows (Bloodaxe Books, 1980)
Watching for Dolphins (Bloodaxe Books, 1983)
Early Greek Travellers and the Hellenic Ideal
  (Cambridge University Press, 1984)
Davies (Bloodaxe Books, 1985)

DAVID CONSTANTINE

Madder

BLOODAXE BOOKS

ISBN: 1 85224 039 3

First published 1987 by
Bloodaxe Books Ltd,
P.O. Box 1SN,
Newcastle upon Tyne NE99 1SN.

Bloodaxe Books Ltd acknowledges
the financial assistance of Northern Arts.

Typesetting by Bryan Williamson, Manchester.

Printed in Great Britain by
Bell & Bain Limited, Glasgow, Scotland

Acknowledgements

Acknowledgements are due to the editors of the following publications in which some of these poems first appeared: *Anglo-Welsh Review*, *Britische Lyrik der Gegenwart* (Forum, 1984), *Firebird 3* (Penguin, 1984), *Footnotes*, *Helix*, *Mandeville's Travellers* (Mandeville Press, 1984), *New Poetry from Oxford*, *New Yorick*, *Oxford Magazine*, *Oxford Poetry*, *People to People*, *PN Review*, *Poetry Book Society Anthology 1987/88* (Hutchinson/PBS, 1987), *Poetry Canada Review*, *Poetry* (Chicago), *Poetry Durham*, *Poetry Review*, *Public Works*, *Times Literary Supplement*, *2 Plus 2*, *Verse* and *Waves*.

'Oranges', 'The Meeting of God and Michael Finnegan in South Park', 'Garden with red-hot pokers and agapanthus' and 'Wet lilac, drifts of hail' were broadcast on *Poetry Now* (BBC Radio 3), and 'Eden Grove N7' was broadcast on the BBC World Service.

Mappa Mundi was published by the Five Seasons Press in 1984.

Contents

I mean the Dyer's Madder, *Rubia tinctorum*, that used to be cultivated extensively in Europe, especially in southern France, where it was called *garance*. The dye they got from it was a deep red, but the plant itself, a straggling, hairy and sharp-leaved plant, is dark green in colour. The flowers are small and yellow, the berries as they form pass from green through red to black, and when ripe they are juicy. The roots are the thing, that is where the redness is, in the thick, proliferating, energetic roots. Madder was planted in July and harvested in November of the following year. It was cleansed of its earth, then hung for months to dry; then ground to a serviceable powder in mills. This powder needed to be used within a year, before its virtue diminished.

Garance occurs as a measure of redness in troubadour poetry. 'His face went redder than madder', they might say – for shame, perhaps, or love or anger. The powder was used against poisons and to heal a wound. And in 1737 an English surgeon by the name of Belcher fed madder to a pig and turned its skeleton red. He fed some to his chickens and turkeys too, and on the third day they were thoroughly red, in bone and tooth and claw. This Belcher fellow made me think of Orpheus.

Adam confesses an infidelity to Eve

I dreamed you were stolen from my left side
And woke hugging the pain. There in our room
Lit by the street lamp she appeared to me
Like something pulled from the earth. She is bulb-white;

Her shadowy place as black as wet moss
Or the widow spider. Believe me
She flattened my raised hands. She gripped
The cage of my heart between her knees,

Gluttonous for mandrake, and fed then,
Crammed her nether mouth, so rooting at
My evasive tongue I feared she would swallow it.
Curtained together under her hair

Only when she rose from drinking
And rolled and bucked as though I were reined
Did I see her face, like a slant moon,
Her eyes smudged and cavernous, her mouth bruised.

She cried like a seal. When she bowed down
Her brow on mine as savages pray
Enshrining my head between her forearms
Then, I confess, feeling her cold tears

I lapped them from her cheeks and let her rest.
My seed ran out of her, cold. On the street
Hissing with rain the lamps were extinguished.
You, when I woke, lay hooped on my left arm.

Orpheus

Styx is only a stone's throw from here,
From anywhere, but listen: here
You can catch Eurydice's scream
And count how long before she hits

That water. Afterwards
He mooched through such a landscape:
The sun was low in the wrong hemisphere
And hurt his eyes, the birds

Were plump and garish and their chorus,
Mornings, a lascivious rattle;
His familiar trees – the willow,
The poplar – were all yellow

But as blanched as what he had seen of the damned
Were the unfamiliar. Through a willow fringe
He watched the people who looked accustomed
Taking their walks and seemed

To himself only as she had seen him last:
A silhouette. Dearest
I think it was such a flight of poplars
He entered finally and turned

At the dazzled end, calico-thin,
And saw his red griefs coming for him. Listen:
The whisper of Styx, her scream
On which his slung head, singing softly, homes.

Siesta

On edge again, over nothing
Near to tears, when the curtain rattles
And only the warm wind enters
And not the scent of rain, he sees

Garance (it is the name of a flower)
Leaving the water as he approaches
And putting on her clothes.
She ages rapidly around the eyes.

Any more songs, he cries, any more stories,
Any more entering as sisters arm in arm
And leading me to believe you in the shuttered room
Barefoot on the marble

And you can look for me in spots of blood
Across the ponds of cotton grass.

Yseut

The white company of the lepers
Whom we pitied a little and left food for
Whose myxy eyes skenned down the misery slit
At our virgins receiving the Saviour

They have a new white queen
And we go out less, nobody picnics, theirs
Are all the pastorals of this season.
What have we done, what have we let happen?

The King's glee was shortlived.
When the gate banged and he heard their jubilation
He turned the colour of the underside of fungus
He was of a weeping texture, feverous.

One of us shot into the pack today
When they were feasting with their blunt hands
At the cressy well. Now their bells
And clappers are louder and we are nervy.

The King stands looking at the lonely post.
He wants her back again in the opened cloak
Of faggots: to see her soul like a water-baby
Scat heavenwards through the smoke.

He will put a bounty on his Queen
And send us hunting the scuttling herds.
He sweats at the thought that she will give birth.
Her progeny, his doing, will people the earth.

Ignis

This land was crazy with the loves of Christ:
Straight running of the lame, a dance,
The multitude picnicking.

Ones he unfastened the mouths of
And got their tongues going
They ran about charged with the word 'ignis',

They babbled to right and left of an interdiction,
Their mouths overflowed
With tongues, with lucifers, and ones

He took out the darkness under the lids from
And told them not to tell
They saw the light of the eyes into everything.

He said to follow his trespasses
And convert the charnel lands
Where our brothers and sisters still go cutting themselves.

Martyr

This man, if we can call him that, this foetus,
This white larva, he was there at the Dry Tree
As a merry child, a pig-minder, when Christ,
So we believe, (the dates do tally) did that
Trick with spittle and two dead eyes and the sight
Or was it the ensuing loud hallelujah
Or being spotted in the stinking mayweed
Tugging away at himself no doubt among
Our burned-out necklaces and the handy stones
And Jesus telling him to cross his heart and
Hope to die if he told a soul about it
(Everyone did) and him telling his mam? It
Blew the wits of that doughty little witness
Of many occurrences on that bloody spot.
His mam never saw the stars of his eyes again.
She watched him curl and eavesdropped on his nightmares.
She even petitioned the travelling Master
To please come and wipe her little man's vision
Clean of the miracle. We reckon in his fist
(Observe how over the years he has eaten at it)
We'll find the crooked sixpence Jesus flicked him
When our blind brother saw the heavenly blue.

Oh, Jemima…

I was there, I was the man in black in case
His ticker burst, but I watched Jemima
Whom they were yelling at to look and the sweet thing
In boots sucked on her barley sugar and throughout
The uproar of the ducks and when our man was in
Rotavating the water with his white arms
And his legs were fighting one another she
Only did as she was bid and looked and of course
Never screamed nor covered her eyes nor wet herself.

She saw him crawl up the bank with muddy eyes
And weed on his tonsure and his busy-bee stripes
At half-mast, Flo handing him his glasses
And a cup of tea and Arthur a handkerchief and me
Going in with my little silver ponce to sound him out.

And I was there coming down from Ethel's bed
And the same little nod our Jemima gave
When they wrapped Uncle away I saw her give
That morning over her bowl when Flo's card came
Saying that Jim, the learner, the brave tryer,
Was took on the West Coast doing his few strokes
Up the Acheron, against its tide, into its freezing mouth.

Don't jump off the roof, Dad...

I see the amplified mouths of my little ones
And dear old Betty beseeching me with a trowel.
I am the breadwinner, they want me down of course.
I expect they have telephoned the fire brigade.

They have misinterpreted my whizzing arms:
I am not losing my balance nor fighting wasps
Nor waving hello nor signalling for help.
These are my props and I am revving up.

From here I have pity on the whole estate.
The homegoing lollipop lady regards me with amazement.
I shall be on the news. Lovely Mrs Pemberton
Will clutch Mr Pemberton and cry: It's him!

Ladies, I am not bandy, it is the footing I must keep.
My run-up along the ridge-tiles will be inelegant.
But after lift-off, breasting the balmy wind
And when I bear westwards and have the wind in my tail

Then what a shot I shall make, going for the big sun,
Over the flowering cherries and the weeping willows,
Beating along Acacia Avenue with a purpose
Towards the park and the ornamental lake.

The Meeting of God and Michael Finnegan in South Park

Sunday, early; foul with dreams
Entering the empty park between two bent railings
I found his crutches towards the bottom of the hill
Lying on the long undulations of grass
Like spars of wreck. So, I thought,
Michael has met God as he always said he would.

He will have dropped from them last night
Having swung this far out of the soiled city.
Here is his jagged bottle. This morning then,
Waking with scabby lips, he saw God walking in the park,
Dewy-grey, delighted by blackbirds and songthrushes
And the scent of the mown grass. Look, God said

To Michael Finnegan, how beautiful the city is,
The white spires, delicate as a moonshell,
Reaching from sleep into the soft blue daylight.
And see the well-spaced leafing trees: that copse
Through which is passing even now a *frisson* of joy,
That single poplar in a brave plume – and there

A damp place which is a beginning stream
To water the pale city. Begin again, said God,
Leave your crutches lying and no excuses. Don't,
For example, be telling me you must wait for the keeper
To let you out. My fence is vandalised
Where you came in and above, higher,

Passing that single and admonishing poplar,
That convocation of oaks, that company
Of beeches downed like youths in Homer,
Leaving behind and further and further below you
The city sparkling like a hoard of shells
You will find a gap I made for the convenience of the children.

So Michael Finnegan spewed up some green bile
And wiped his lips and saw blood on the back of his hand
And found his feet and climbed the long slope unaided
And far below him in the moonlike city
From towers, faintly, fell the notes
Of an hour that was still unearthly.

Don Giovanni: Six Sonnets

1 *Act 2 Scene 18*

When he had gone, burning in hell fire,
And the valet in black had drawn the cloth and they
Had sung the restoration of order in a choir
In separate silences they turned loosely away:
Facing a nunnery, marriage to a fool, marriage
To a woman in love and service more tedious.
He was their sun, his fist had held them, each
Released now travelled down a different radius.

Turning on a widening wheel, come spring
After a winter they will rake his fires to life
Under the heart's ash and his singing will begin again
Coursing through them like sap. Thirsting then, burning,
Servant, nun, husband, unloving wife
Will scan the linen for his last wine's stain.

2 *'How can men want wearisomely to philander?'*
Leporello to Donn' Elvira

Burgos is full of women and Burgos is only one
Of the cities of Spain full of women and Spain
Etc. They are a drop in the ocean
The thousand and three. And it's all labour in vain.
He's ladling at women with a sieve
And like the proverbial good shepherd he'll leave
The one to chase the missing ninety-nine
Up hill down dale in the wind and the rain
And lose the one. Lady, he never lets up.
The poor man hasn't had a holiday in years.
He sees himself as one of life's almoners
And bringers of sunshine, handing his loving cup
To rich and poor, fair and ugly, and the shriven
Kneeling with sinners for his French stick of heaven.

3 *Zerlina*

Waking this morning I was someone else:
A wife who knows she has conceived, but the shock
I felt under my heart was remembering how he struck
The strings with the backs of his fingers and my new pulse
Was the starting again of his singing in my veins
Sotto voce. I have gone about the house
And to and fro in the garden hearing his damned voice
All day under my clothes carrying his tunes.

He swung my soul, he showed me how they move
In very presence, those whom an innocent love
Flings to the dance. And I believed his tongue,
I swallowed him, we married there and then.
I am his lawful widow big with song.
I have danced all day, believing him again.

4 *Zerlina*

He had a house, if I would follow him in
He promised we should debate the old question
How many angels might dance on the head of a pin
He guessed in my case more than a million.
There was music for what we felt, he said,
But as yet no dance. I was to imagine
Things overlapping, things deeply interlaid,
Crown-knots of fire. His hand on mine,
Our fingers so interslotted that we could not tell
Left from right, his from mine. I was to dwell
As dance on the interleaving of warm waves
Over a sand bar, their passing through themselves,
Their continuing rippling on the tide that weaves
A depth of them in which the island dissolves.

5 *Leporello*

Forked in her moorish arches, standing sentry,
I watched the summer heavens teeming down;
I dozed under her generous balcony,
Dopey with orange blossom and moonshine,
Hearing their silly laughter above my head,
His rapier clattering to the marble floor,
Rustle and sigh of things of hers discarded,
A rose thrown over into my lamplight square.
When he came down I kissed his ungloved hands
And we escaped then through the skirting gardens.
Once, in the wolf's clothing, using his voice,
I drew his starved wife down. Inhaled the perfume
Of an amorous woman, saw the abandoned face
That hurt my eyes even through my borrowed plume.

6 *Donn' Elvira*

I see my face in the black window glass;
I touch my throat, feeling for Christ's chain;
I think of charitable casual women
Who at the throat begin to undo their dress.

Christ knows my visions and may forgive me them.
They are of women and my spouse in Hell.
They stand among their fallen clothes and smile
And show him their white places without shame.

I should have smiled, I should have had their ease.
My love was like the terror of the lamb
Under his knife. Don Juan never saw
Amusement at his passion in my eyes.
I am the widow of a man at whom
I never smiled as though I were his whore.

Idylls

Prologue

Pan speaks these things
On behalf of his surviving friends:
A dumb goat, dumber
Goatherd and a poor
Battered Priapus – Pan
Whose decease was announced off Paxos
To Thamus, an Egyptian,
Across the water when
The love of Christ began.

Goat

i.

I like my tableland,
My level, and my rope's length
Of circumference around the stump.
Silvery-grey-green
The light trickles over my head
And I can sniff the sea.
Every day a bird
Trills like delirium when the sun
Strikes her through the bars.
Now and then a sister comes
Leading a she as white
As fetta handed from the tub.
The sister and I are black.
They stay. Before they leave
The furious hanged bell
Will have given its summons up.

ii.

One night my yellow eye
Observed the men of St Basil
Ascending the terraces, skirts
Hitched, in Indian file.
There was no alarum. Soon
The house giggled. And once
At crackling noon, my chin
On the broken earth, I saw
The white feet coming
That are a cause for panic.
I would not look up. But I watch
The man who digs for the sister
Enjoying a tree-hole
Bunged with figs. I swear
The gnarled trunk bucks.

iii.

A town comes down
To sherds and bones. A man
Can't shuffle for purchase here
But the old back legs
Rake up somebody's handle,
Spout, fondled curves
Or delicate red horn.
Bad days when they came
And lopped off the bells to dangle
Christians there, and the heads,
Countless heads,
Every one different,
Leaped my heavenly stairs
Through the olive branches'
Pleasance. Then the choked
Torrents disgorged and the sea
That carried the ark, and Mary
On a moon and naked love
On a shell, the poor sea
Blushed through the shallows to her depths.

[Chios]

26

Priapus

Nobody visits but
That humpy man and birds
Who shit on my head. The nights
Fall, days break
And I'm still here by the heap
Where the man is fattening a thing
For Mother Superior. My knob
Got knocked off long ago
By Saint Someone, a hot
Fat pederast. Such fun
I had in the old days
And never moved, it was never
Me to blame but young
And old of the two sexes
Came with oily hands
And cups of honey and climbed
The way they liked and for beasts too
I was a rubbing post,
I shone down there
Like Peter's toe, young girls
First got the hang of it
By me and men as twisted
As olives spat on their palms
For the old good luck.

[Chios]

Goatherd

i.

Under the wrecked eeries
Of cracked ascetics
Among my chiming beasts
At noon I put up my prick
And call Deutschland.

Weekends away
Under the dirty mags;
The kino stills; that place
You were feasted privately like dunces
On a spread of the real thing
Spot-lit; shows;
And when the caravan came
How silently we queued
Twice round the yard.

ii.

On fine Sundays
We mooched in the park, the girls
Were sauntering with Germans,
But very often it rained
All weekend
We lay on our bunks until
It was time to watch a train
Pull out or see
Somebody off with his goods:
Hi-fi, Omo
In giant packets, a bike
For the boy. I used to remember
Father in his cave and the nights
I slept up there, the stink
Was homely, the river
Made a beautiful din
With the nightingales
To sleep to. I remembered that once
I woke and thought Elijah
Was climbing the spurs home
On the far side all
Silver and our one eye,
The fire in the black cave,
Guided him and he blessed us.

[Meteora/Olympus]

28

Confessional

Where, in a French church, stuck through
And dreaming of haymaking in Liebenau,
Should he go to die? Not in the lee of the altar
Nor spreadeagled under the tower.
He hid in the confessional and died seated
Leaning forward as though to the priest's ear.

Americans were brought in dead
And laid down the hollow nave to the altar steps
And from north to south on the transept
And peasants with faces like the Conqueror's
Embarking in their church windows made
A white cross over them with armfuls of June flowers.

The dead man from Liebenau sat still
Behind the curtain in the confessional
Pressing his open mouth to the grille.

Thoughts of the Commandant of the Fortress
of St Vaast-la-Hougue

My boy keeps up appearances.
He props the dead soldiers in their embrasures
And fires their muskets from time to time.

By candle light in the nucleus
With a bitten finger I patrol our miles of walls
Hearing at every turn the claws of a grapnel
Or the moat bleeding away through a wound.

And what is worse: low tide when we
Padlock our throat and cordon the slit with salt
And the birds stalk over the foetid mud
Bayoneting the overturned soft crustaceans?

Or full: when we are brimming with fear
That our besiegers thus will fall quietly upon us
With the soft wings and the demon faces of moths?

They have surrendered oceans of freedom to beat these walls.
How furious will be their disappointment
After the falling silent of my ragged bird-scarer.

Pillbox

Dome of the sun. So we shall burn
Immured in a head, peering through hyphens.
Though we are prickly with angles of vision
An intelligence may calculate our blindspots
A hand rise out of the earth
To post us flames. Somebody squats
On the skull with a trepan
Where our flailing glances cannot dislodge him.
The surf is placid at nights
And soothing the scent of camomile.
We have nailed this coast. Buried to the eyeballs
We shall burn like lampions.
The quenching Atlantic will back away from us.

Nestor encourages the troops
(after Iliad *ii. 336ff.)*

My dears, you sound like little boys
Still pimply before they redden out
With bloodlust. Who promised then? Did not
We all with drink and a handshake
Cross our hearts and hope to die
For Agamemnon? Yapping, though we yap
Till kingdom come, will get us nowhere. Sir,
Lead them cheerfully back on to
The killing-ground and let
The one or two malingerers, the schemers
For early home-time, the impiously
Unwaiting to hear God's final word, let them
Drop dead. I personally
Believe we were given the nod and the wink
That day by Zeus. It lightened, did it not,
Righthandedly when we were boarding
Our snouted ships for Troy. Well then
For Helen's misdemeanours and your wasted years
Anticipate a just desert
Of married Trojan cunt. When we are in
And the pretty fires are burning and only toddlers
And snivelling old men encumber your knees
Remember then you thought of going home. However
If luxury to come (shitting on silks)
Will not embolden you try running and we,
Your lords, will stick you to the ships.

Garden with red-hot pokers and agapanthus

The link flowers that stood in a loose sheaf
Cock-red and yellow-wattled
A clear honey dabbling their waxy spikes

When you pushed open the gate in the garden wall
They dubbed your bare shoulder
When you went down the granite steps

Pushing open the gate that was always half-open
You agitated the flames and the embers
When you went down into the cool agapanthus.

The green iron gate was always half-open,
There were three steps down. The agapanthus
Is shock-headed and slim. Love, through a caul,

Through slung cells dotted with life,
Through sunrises and rose
Windows of webs I watched for you climbing

Out of the place of quenched fires
Dew on your hair, your flinching shoulders
Touched with yellow pollen.

'Looking for nothing'

Looking for nothing but a place in the sun
We found the cricket-pitch that nobody
Finds by looking: an outfield head-high,
A plateau of curious topiary
And twenty-two paces of asphalt battened on
By gorse like sea-slugs. Over the boundary

The wind streamed downhill in a bright sunlight
Through choppy bracken with a watery din
And entered the sea. Wading in
We found the drinking trough of lichened concrete
Still holding water that had fallen sweet
Nowhere arable, nowhere beasts might feed.

We lay in the sun's cupped hands
By the undrunk water mouth on mouth
Below the cricketers' flat earth, beyond
Their lost sixes. We opened
Rapidly from diminutive springs, like breath
Surfacing butterflies wafted down the wind.

Sunset Shells

Sunset shells, of which there were millions
Banked at our bare feet, like a flint scraper
They fit exactly into an idle
Skimming grip between finger and thumb.

That day whilst the sun blew and the long-
Sleeved tide harped louder over the sandbar
Until the island was awash for the last
Half hour we were launching sunset shells.

Oh, we threw thousands, they saucered up and
Cut from under by the sunny wind
Each at its curve's high-point paused spinning
And was returned overhead into

The sea's incoming arms with a sound
Like kissing and floated briefly, we had
Behind us a flotilla of little
Sinking coracles and in the sky

Always any number climbing to
Their points of stall and boomeranging down
The windslopes. The sun laughed and the tide
Like clapping drew the last white curtains.

Oranges

i.

Mother has linen from the *Minnehaha*,
I bought the ship's bell for half a sovereign
From Stanley, our dumb man.
Everyone has something, a chair, a bit of brass

And nobody wakes hearing a wind blow
Who does not hope there'll be things come in
Worth having, but today
Was a quiet morning after a quiet night.

ii.

The bay was coloured in
With bobbing oranges. What silence
Till we pitched into it
Knee-deep the women holding out their skirts

And the men thrashing in boats
We made an easy killing
We took off multitudes
And mounded them in the cold sun.

When Matty halved one with his jack-knife
It was good right through, as red
As garnet, he gave the halves
His girls who sucked them out.

iii.

The beams we owe the sea
Are restless tonight but every home
Is lit with oranges. They were close,
She says, or else the salt

Had eaten them. Whose popping eyes,
I wonder, saw them leave
Roaring like meteors
When the ship in a quiet night

Bled them and they climbed
Faster than rats in furious shining shoals
In firm bubbles and what
Will tumble in our broken bay tomorrow?

Sols

(for Alice Thomas, in memory of her son,
my cousin, who died in 1943, aged three weeks)

1

Planting is hard, so much stooping uphill,
But leisurely and we can lob
Some conversation over the high hedges,
Share forenoon in a strip of shade.

Picking is desperate though, the wind
Reaches in like a bear fishing.
We get them out earlier and earlier
Hurrying under frightful red skies.

The market demands it, however green
They are and tighter than shut beaks.
Packing them is a stiff business,
So many rods, box after box. Some die,

That's certain, die at sea, and what
Could we deal worse into the roofed homes
There to be broached behind drawn curtains
Than a Christmas box of sols

With wrinkled eyes that no one's hands
Taking them up or water will freshen?
The house had already imagined
The scent of gratefulness in every room

Which is the breathing again of sols
When a woman lifts them like a love child
Out of the ark that crossed the wolfish sea
From the world's end at the time of miracles.

2

The harvests were golden once and every room
Of that formal maze had a fire of flowers
Whatever the weather constantly fuelled
With cradled armfuls. The little paths

Going through our roofless windy city
Like cracks in brickwork by two or three steps
At slits in the tall euonymus
Trickled with gold. The trundling carts

Climbed to the packing-house, the long shed,
Like royal hearses. From a broken rim
The harboured steamer received into her hold
The burden of busy gigs and launches.

3

They worked all the hours God gave
They could never pick fast enough
The fingers of the women were raw with tying
They were minting gold
Hand over fist, the currency of grief,
And bloating the steamer with condolences.

4

Christmas, and not a candle showing;
The steamer kept coming, the markets of London
Were lit with flowers, by grief's
Osmosis they were drawn

Through every capillary:
Down highways in a slow march
Sinuously through lanes and cricked
At stepping angles through the slums.

5

Put off alone in a white ark
He scents the room like bread
Fresh on a board, like sols
In sparkling vases. But silence is natural
To the breathing of bread and sols and nobody
Pushing open the door ajar
On darkness would listen thus and crane
And tiptoe in and lean with an ear downwards
To be certain they still lived.

6 *Strafe*

Curiosity, since by daylight
He could never revisit the unroofed slums
To peer inside or glance at a slice of living-room –
Its tatters of floral wallpaper and dog's

Hind-leg of a flue – he never saw
In a winter daylight the exact layout
Of our cemetery fixed among the lines
Of railway, box-like factories and canal,

Never swooped low in the sparkling frostlight
To observe the neat little casts of the newest graves
And their cut flowers and perhaps a cortège
Pushing, as though congealing, through a back street.

So curiosity brought him low over the bulbfields,
Gentle township of evergreen walls,
Corrals of sunshine open to the sky
Whose goods nothing worse than a south-easter swipes.

And there were little people busy at the source of flowers
Who ran at his roar, dropping their burdens,
And hid where we look for shade.
He came in low, he saw their white faces.

7

Since it is sleep that makes possible
The coming of the sackman, cherry-red,
Who can pass through soot with his white beard immaculate,
Sleep and the darkness, a black heaven,

A sheeted firmament, darkness in the attic,
Darkness in all the sleeping rooms,
The children are desperate to sleep and clench their eyes
Fearful they keep the red man listening at the door

Unable to enter, fearful he will turn on his heel
And shoulder the sack, but worse, almost,
Should he mistakenly believe their breathing
And enter the knowing darkness with effulgent whiskers.

8

Concave over the magic box
My father holds his breath and a small soul
Has appeared in the Brownie eye. Then light
Admitted is severed with a click.

Soon I am entered in the quilted album
On the first black page. All babies look alike
But here is my name in small white capitals.
Ergo sum! My resting place

Is the Morrison built not to give
At the knees or cave in under
A rubbled house. It easily took
Your leaden grief in a box till he

Was sided away to a third-class plot
In the big necropolis
In perpetuity. Lid the cradle
And that is how it looked, with flowers,

In a blacked-out house when he had flitted through
The lit rooms, your cock sparrow.
But you had pictured him for ever.
As we go forward now

Print after print and you are saying what
He would have been, I blur with light
Like streetlamps when our eyes are wet
As if his ghost got in.

9

Had he come down from the dark
Even three or four of the fifteen stairs
He could have looked into the living-room
And seen the fire and the lord of the fire:

Father in a long dressing-gown,
A shield on his arm, the black blower;
A sword in his hand, the silver poker;
Ushering the flames up. When Father kneeled

And tinkered with the damper
The flames became a quiet curtain
This side of which there was a smell of hot soot
And a trail of Woolworth's glitter.

Hugging the cornucopia,
The lumpy stocking from the bed-end,
Had he come in the table was laid for him
Its leaves extended as though for company.

Crusaders in a fort; a farm:
The lovable animals, the health of the green fields;
Houses, a lighted church, the whole world
Looped by a tremendous locomotive.

[St Martin's, Isles of Scilly / Salford 5]

42

Cold Night

We saw the pent fish redden the ice
In a Grecian park where the Cnidian
And Pan accustomed to nightingales
Stayed out all night with the owls.

The trees are brittle, the streams wrung dry;
The ice yelps at the least thing
Like a railway line; along
The scoured road there are drifts in a drove.

Drifts: they are water thrown
Under the undulating air, they are
The manifest line breath took
When the clouding water set. And we

Where are we? Listening to the owls
Or the ice or the rim of the moon:
Something that cries with little cries
Under the lake moon, under the ice

Where the drifts move in their shapes
Like seals or whales and sound
For one another down the bloodstreams
With a strange phoning, like owls.

'As though on a mountain'

As though on a mountain, on the sunny side,
The view over seven counties suddenly palled
And the stream we had bathed in, our loveliest,
We fell to damming so that not the least
Of relief could leak through, no not a mouthful;

As though downstream somewhere, still naked,
We seated ourselves on the two facing rocks
And made some conversation until the air tasted,
The shallows got tepid and our mouths dried up
And we listened to the waters piling behind our backs;

As though we joined hands then, still bleeding from the labour;
As though the waters broke; as though together
With rubble and furious fish and trees the chute
Of waters shovelled us off the mountain
Eating each other's heart in the mouth out.

To be honest, I'm losing my nerve. One day
We'll finish in town like that, on show,
A phenomenon come out of the sky, beastly,
My beautiful, ingrown, rooted through.

At Dinas

The sea runs, the long-haired breakers
Come on and on with a constant thunder;
They wear the pelts and manes of animals,
They show their throats.

At the sea's edge you look run to death,
You turn your face towards us shining with tears,
You seem to hang from your surrendering wrists;
But the sea lifts

As though you raised it. For if grief tears
The head back so will happiness, the throat
Intones and maybe your mouth's drowned
O is singing.

We three look monstrous, our heads so close
The blood beats through and across our open mouths
The wind howling. But thus we accompany you
With drum and flute.

Local Story

i.

When a tree falls
The rooty place
Is beloved of children.
We opened loaves
And fruit for one another;
At the tap-root
Drank a white drink.
All we asked was to flower
In one another's features
And be apportioned
Fairly below.

ii.

To the black cwm
Through the sunny forest
By way of the stream.
Though I often turned
You continued following
Bare to the waist
You three were following.

A grey snow
Hurts in the cracks of the face
Long beyond spring;
Scree, wreckage,
A circling echo.
Where have I led you
Shivering?

iii.

Reading the excreta
Of crows and foxes
We fell on whortleberries.
We had inky fingers
And the mouths of the drowned.

On a high headland
In a form of heather
We entertained the lord of the place
Old Proteus
With our curious love-knots.

The light changed
The hill stood up and brushed our picnic off.
God watched us out of sight with other clouds.
We were never hived
We were less than crumbs of pollen.

iv.

We lit a last fire with our swag of seed.
Under the coals
Among the kindling of splintered driftwood
It sang and cried.
We swallowed souls of firelight in our wine.

Mynydd Mawr

All night sopping up rain
At daybreak the wells of the hill opened
The animal in my crystal valley
Doled itself downstream more rapidly.

Everything flows, it must, the skull
That lodges in the stream exults
At the eyes and at the widened mouth. On Mynydd Mawr
A high wind bearing the law upon me

I let this house go, turning it
Into the rivers from the rainbow's end
Let go our beds and fires
The bowl of berries and the driftwood in arms

The holly, the harebells and the only rowan
And the long icicles brought home
I dealt them down the wind
I conjured everything out of me

Owls and curlews and a peck of jackdaws
And the tunes of dreams. Turning then
There was a steady scintillation
The wet was shining off every surface stone

As I came into the quick of the rainbow
Into the roar with widening eyes
And over my thin skin Mynydd Mawr
Flowed out of the sky, cold silver.

Swimmer

(in memoriam Frances Horovitz, 1938-83)

In summer the fires come and feed here
Like starlings. If the earth knew
She would feel a shiver of memory.
Ash on that crumpled ground.

The lake in a luminous silence, sunlight
Shed generally through the air,
A light of dreams; no lapping, shingle and
Water in a still seam.

Swimmer, the hills say, having come through ash
And snagging stumps and now
Idling on a warm surface to the midpoint
Naked, alone, try standing,

Swimmer, the sky says, tread water and feel
How thin the warmth is, thinner
Than the earth's burned hide, as thin as the Holocene
On Time's shaft and below

What a pull of cold, what colder than stone depths
Your feet are rooting in
And the cold rising as though cold were the sap
And blood of a new flower:

Death. Try calling a name, swimmer at the hub
Of a lake in a wheel
Of hills, your voice will flutter on the black slopes.
Kick, then, enjoy the surface.

Butterfly

A year and a day. Then too
There were daddy-long-legs wrecked on the flagstones
And ladybirds heading nowhere.

He offered me something in his closed hands
So suddenly my breath came with a scream.
He said was I frightened even of butterfly kisses?
Did I think he would feed me a spider?

He looked bound at the wrists
Until the flower of his hands opened
And he showed her spread and gave her up to the sky
With whole days still to live.

Fly away home: the poor shell creatures cannot
Nor can the crippled dancers lift
Off these immense piazzas.

'Then comes this fool'

Then comes this fool, muttering about freedom
And stands watching my hands and makes me nervous
And says there's a better game he knows with hands
And undoes everything, and what *he* does

Looks complicated, like a cat's-cradle,
And frail as a web and more and more like a rainbow
When he makes that wicked sign with his thumbs and fingers
And purses his lips and softly begins to blow.

And I'll set sail, he says, there's a nice breeze,
I'll probably be in paradise by tea-time.
I ask what the life expectancy of bubbles is.
They go far, he says. He says in the first dream

When I had hidden he was only passing
And kissed my whitened knuckles on the window bars.
I wonder how I undo what it was he did.
He will push off soon, muttering about the stars.

Mistress

Women whose hands know the feel of a baby's head
Push them confidently in among the melons
And their strong brown thumbs side by side,
Beautifully cuticled, feel for give on the crown.

That summer of the hot winds and the fires
The melons were sold split. He held me one
Before we had paid for it, before all the people,
To smell the inside of at its small
Opening fleur-de-lys and we went down
In a river of laughter between the banked stalls
Among all the people swinging our fruit in a net.

He made the cuts but I opened it
And for a moment my hands were a bowl of flames.
I served him cradles and the moons of nursery rhymes
And a family of rocking boats. We ate
And our mouths ran over with luscious smiles.

Then he closed my hands into a fist and held them shut.

'Wet lilac, drifts of hail'

Wet lilac, drifts of hail; everything shines
After the white rain, the gutters stream with seed;
Glistening in a fierce sun the road pitches
Downhill into an entrance of chestnut trees.

Tonight shall we cross the same meadow
And steal in the long gardens? I wore
Blossom in my hair, I wore a white dress,
I gave him my shoes to carry and ran away barefoot.

In love's month, after the first winter,
Apple trees revive in the memory of the dead
And they remember pink and white apple blossom
Flung down on the grass like a girl's clothes.

After a year the entrance is lit again
With high candles and the dead wait in the dark
For somebody coming, their flowers of hope
Plucking to nothing in fretting fingers.

My empty-handed love, someone will come
Soon bringing me armfuls of stolen lilac,
Sparkles of rain in his hair, and the black earth
Tonight when I run barefoot will quake with sobs.

Poplar

He slept at once as though
Escaping, he slid from my mouth
With a smile of thankfulness
And at the temple then his blood
Quietened upon my heartbeat, as though
The sea had pitched him far enough
And now withdrew, but I
Came to and heard
What I thought was a river
Passing overhead through our crown
Of leaves, I seemed
To be lying in a downpour, one
That drenched and blessed
My sleepy sub-self, the ground
Of me, and I wondered at
His fear of sadness
And of new desire like that
For snowy mountains rising again
Always too far distant,
I could conceive of none –
No thirst, no sadness, no distance –
My downpour could not answer.

Apples
(for my father-in-law on his eightieth birthday)

The daughter has a taste for sharp apples
And lolls in a fork, munching; little brother,
Blonder than corn, can dangle one-handed
Far out. Elsewhere, so I believe,

These things are forbidden, there is a scarecrow
And it is not you who strolls by
To see what the children are up to
But old Mr McGregor or God the Father.

On the lawn all you are judging
Is the likely parabola of apples when the tree
With a shout next fires one off;
You resemble a Green Man

Fielding eagerly at silly-point,
Your nettle-proof hands seem to be praying
Apples will fall. Those we miss
Bruise with a white spittle

And some my ring nicks, we lay them down
For immediate pies. In the apple light
Among the globes and leaves
The lucky children have ascended again

To the era of pure monkey tricks
Where lichen roughened us
And we were barked and greened. Our little Lob
Has stuffed his tee shirt full

So that I wonder, and perhaps you do too,
Who are four yards and forty years away,
Whether apples in a shirt
Have the feel girls have. Catching apples

And once my daughter's core
All afternoon I have been praising Eve,
The starred girl, the apple-halver,
Who has redeemed us from Mary-without-spot.

London Road

Even the signpost's gone
That stood here pointing which way
London was and the miles,
One hundred and eighty-six,

With a finger. Then the road
Smiled and hitched up its pants
And put its best foot forward
And sloughed all this here off:

The blinded warehouses,
The shops doing badly,
The chapels doing worse, the big
Empty Majestic, all the slag.

For the road believed
The friendly hand and the pointing finger
Their definite number of miles
And shouldered its bundle on a stick.

Yes, said the standing post,
In the voice of a blackened elder,
There's nothing but fields now,
You'll get your strength up marching,

You'll get some air, you'll be fit
For the folks in London to look at.
Go on, son, you can do it,
Though none of us ever did.

Eden Grove N7

In the end it was only merciful
To lid them over, they were an eyesore
And seemed themselves no longer
To wish to be looked at by the sun.

And are they dead? No, no,
They live in the darkness, hurt,
The rats fret them and everything that falls
Comes their way. We seep through.

Pity the waters and do not imagine
That in time they will run clean again
And visit with refreshment
The sickening roots of our brave trees;

Nor that, stopped here, they will shout up elsewhere
One fine day; nor that
All along under the concrete
They are undermining us with the old joy.

Here instead is an old fool
Who remembers it was all fields
Round here when he was a boy
And that he lay in the silverspoons

Counting larks. And here is another,
Half his age, who says
Not long ago with a heavy coin
You could get out of here and caper all day

On golden sands and eat
A speciality out of a paper bag
And ride home again under a merry sky
Jingling the heavy change. They say, they say...

Pictures

Whether to take down the Kissing Swallows
And the Modigliani nude
And blu-tack something else there: a child,
Say, on fire and running towards us

Down a long road; or this little dot
Who bellywise looks almost bigger
Than her mother was; or any
One of those solemn witnesses we stand

In our photographs of a new mass grave
Like gentlemen in an old print
Modestly indicating by their smallness
Something phenomenal. The children

In this photograph from El Salvador
Are that international pair, a boy
And a little girl on a roadsign
Running, and below them, his head

In the gutter and his black blood
Being lapped by a row of dogs, on a road
Empty but for the photographer
A man has fallen among worse than thieves.

Amber Seahorse
(for Mary-Ann)

Europe is ripped through, my darling,
The resinous trees have little spastic arms,
The golden routes are leaden and the lap
He came from can't imbibe much more. I read

That the hippocamp is a sovereigne remedie
Against the byting of a madde dogge. Hold on
To him, it may soon come to that as
Every day they open up more badlands,

Burnish him, love, for some fluorescence
A while longer and note his canny eye,
His long shrewd nose and the springy tail
He rode the flood out on.

Traveller, bright thinker,
Remember the wreckage of the woman of Sindhos
Lying under glass like Snow White
And the finds where they were found:

Amber where the throat was, given her,
I think, and worn for love; a bowl
Lying in her vanished lap, her dusty
Hands had grasped it, proffering.

Poem on my birthday for Irina Ratushinskaya

We have the day in common, also verses;
And the cold has lasted beyond what is usual;
By now there should be coltsfoot. Cold?
It hurts the face a little, the eyes weep perhaps,
But you should see my son brake his toboggan broadside,
You should kiss my bright-eyed daughter cycled home.

Some things are black and white: laws against poems,
A camp on the driven snow. Do the guards enquire
Through the eyes of the line of unspeaking women
Who harbours your verses now? I have read of such cold
That the breath you breathe makes a starry whisper,
It forms on the air, it crackles like interference.

What have you done? They can question you to death,
They can feed your lungs with ice, they can dose
The freely riding waves of the air with dust.
You imprinted the dirty glass with frost gardens,
You muttered of love along the nissen corridors.
Oh triumph of breath! Oh manifest beauty of breathing!

Just now in the dark, turning a year older,
I heard the rain begin. Soon in our country
The little horns of lilac will butt at the sky.
Our house warms through its pipes. The whisper of rain,
A continuous whispering of verses. Courage,
Sister. Good courage, my white sister.

[4 March 1986]

Eldon Hole

They fastened a poor man here on a rope's end
And through the turbulence of the jackdaws let him down
To where everything lost collects, all the earth's cold,
And the crying of fallen things goes round and round
And where, if anywhere, the worm is coiled.

When he had filled with cold they hauled him up.
The horrors were swarming in his beard and hair.
His teeth had broken chattering and could not stop
Mincing his tongue. He lay in the rope and stared,
Stared at the sky and feared he would live for ever.

Like one of those dreadful fish that are all head
They saw him at his little window beaming out
Bald and whiskerless and squiddy-eyed
He hung in the branches of their nightmares like a swede.
They listened at his door for in his throat

Poor Isaac when the wounds in his mouth had healed
Talked to himself deep down. It was a sound
Like the never-ending yelps of a small stone
Falling to where the worm lives and the cold
And everything hurt goes round and round and round.

Sunken Cities

(for Lynne Williamson)

Some wrecks the fish steer clear of and no
Life at all will inhabit them; others
Are cheerful tenements. Since you told me
Of dolphins living in sunken cities

On any blue clear day I imagine them
Arriving here and circling the spires
Slowly like eagles and down the standing
Canyons going faster than bicycles.

For rubble will not do. We must sink entire
Like Ladybower under the reservoir
Or under the two oceans that collide
Around the Wolf and under our ships'

Black shadows Lyonesse. After snow
When the white dome and Saint Mary the Virgin
Look frail on the sky and the gardens
Are blank and silent and sometimes

At evening when the great libraries
Light up like lanterns we are fittest perhaps
For the seabed and to open our doors
And windows to the incoming dolphins.

Landscape with friends

It was like hands when they extend
To greet us or offer fruit in a bowl
Or release a dove. The sun unclasped
And we admired the mountain in a new light.

It was the hour of the very long shadows
Pointing nowhere across the big fields
When the cypresses tap the darkness under the earth.
The fleece of forest on the mountain bloomed.

The gesture of the sun was almost sorrowful
Over the heads of our joy, as though
We missed the point. I praise the light,
I praise the mountain too that had

A self to show, but mostly I praise you
Little enough in the empty field against
That sea-green hill who stood your ground
Embracing and showing me your lighted faces.

At Kirtlington Quarry
(for Simon)

Catch, cricketer. Another year or so
Before you love the fit of a lampshell
Its promontory and pedicle hole
Quite the way I do

Or a section of the honey golden bed
Where the molluscs are lying as thick as leaves
Puts you in mind of Jews in chamber graves
Horribly impacted.

On the old floor, innocent and loveless,
Shapes were shapes, the lampshells swayed
Like nothing but themselves. We made
All the analogies.

Two hundred million years above us
The shape comes, ahead of its roar;
Seems too heavy to float on the surface air;
Has amazing slowness.

Lampshells shining in the oolitic snow;
Stars above all. The guards took bars to prise
The families apart. Here comes the noise
And shadow over you.

Tea-time

Tea-time. Instead of the tea-lady
Enter Aquarius. Fish, she says,
Marry me quickly. Backs the door to.
He sits like Piffy on the window-sill

Knowing she can see behind him, head-high,
Her river with its chunks of ice, stiff sheep
And the homes of fussy coots
Turned upside down. Do it, she says.

Handling the tiller of the tall window
He lets in the din and smell of the black melt.
In her bright eyes he is riding high in the stern
Of a ship of fools. Then the books lift,

The strict papers and the tight-arsed files
They flutter, they butterfly,
They snow up the room like doves, beating it to
The slitted window. Yes, she says, oh yes.

He has an ear for discipline. He hears
The lift land Mrs W.   Girl, he says,
Hold that door handle tighter than Katy did.
Oh come, she says, we shall be gone, she says.

NOTES
Piffy: a creature of indeterminate character and sex.
Mrs W.: the tea-lady.
Katy: the brave Scots girl, Kate Barlass, who bolted the door with
her arm to save her king.

Burning

i.

Brick tholos, heat
Humming about it in a strong sun.

She served in the dough
By a long handle. Bread
On the air, we lay
Idly in the camomile.

ii.

Thatch, it burned;
The doors puffed open, the panes
Shattered like that woman's spectacles
On the Odessa Steps.
Bread had gone into the oven.
It burned.

Tashes of ferns for the pigs' bedding,
Hay for the cattle
Burned. The gorse in flames,
The broom ravelled to nothing;
The heather crackled.

What a squeaking of shrews.

iii.

At low tide we entered a sea-cave.
There it was cold, fireless.
On the sea, as in an old perspective,
We saw charred little boats.

When the sea came home
We backed into the gullet,
Admired the vehemence of past tides
That had so rammed things in.
We remembered a picnic above:

How the sea thumped the air
And the ground blew cheerfully.

He felt for us.
Above the boulder choke
There was a small breathing space.

iv.

Our land is bumpy with tumuli.
The fire uncovered them.
Looters came
With bars and rooted at a blocked entrance
Or stove in the crown.
They will have found
Poor skeletons
No gold
A little earthenware.

v.

The fire blew into the sea.
The black earth raised innumerable foxgloves
Where in living memory there had been none.

We used to think the willowherb came in with the bombs
There followed such a flowering on the sites.

vii.

Into the dunce's cap
Inserting your little finger
Which is the little-bird-told-me
The listening finger
Inserting Baby Small
Under that snuffer
Wish, child,
Wish hard.

'We visit the house'

We visit the house: two blackened gable-ends
Their bedroom fallen in. They had perfected
The gift of lying still and sharing breath
Under one roof their tongues necking in silence,

He in her, fled to a small bud, inside,
Under her thatch, her lintel-bone, her capstone,
Shut-eyed, hibernated, and neither knowing
Exactly where it was, in whom, in what,

A new springwater was divined and roots
Struck quietly. Had they lain apart
They would have heard the low clouds tearing and
The fleeing constellations crying out.

Mother and Daughter

Mother and daughter were found standing
Unharmed in the bloody arena
On stage in the stepped hoofprint
Packed in mud. They had survived

A long bombardment of hot stones
And days of ash. They were found by feelers
Put out choking from a new well-shaft
Sunk for a villa riding high

Among sweet fields. Gently, gently
Resurrected they were thought to be vestals
But no, for certain, they are the mother and
Persephone still dumb from kissing Death.

Nobody loved the earth better than Demeter did
Who trailed it miserably
Calling after her child and nobody's gifts
Withheld were more pined after.

Mother and daughter passed north
From prince to prince and latterly
Survived the fire in Dresden. How Pompeii
Seen from the air resembles sites of ours:

Roofless, crusty. Look where Persephone
Wound in rags
Leads blinded Demeter by the hand
Seeking an entrance to preferable Hades.

The quick and the dead at Pompeii

I cannot stop thinking about the dead at Pompeii.
It was in the Nagasaki and Hiroshima month.
They did not know they were living under a volcano.
Their augurers watched a desperate flight of birds
And wondered about it in the ensuing silence.

There was sixty feet of ash over Pompeii.
It was seventeen centuries before they found the place.
Nobody woke when the sun began again,
Nobody danced. The dead had left their shapes.
The mud was honeycombed with the deserted forms of people.

Fiorelli recovered them by a method the ancients
Invented for statuary. When he cast their bodies
And cracked the crust of mud they were born again
Exactly as they had died. Many were struck
Recumbent, tripped, wincing away, the clothing

Rolled up their backs. They were interrupted:
A visiting woman was compromised for ever,
A beggar hugs his sack, two prisoners are in chains.
Everyone died as they were. A leprous man and wife
Are lying quietly with their children between them.

The works of art at Pompeii were a different matter.
Their statues rose out of mephitic holes bright-eyed.
The fresco people had continued courting and feasting
And playing mythological parts: they had the hues
Of Hermione when Leontes is forgiven.

Fogou

We are watching the sky in a certain quarter
For the look of iron. The house we leave
May be hospitable with the smell of baking bread
When we enter the ground again at the ferny hole.

What pity we shall extend into the sunlight
For our molested rooms, and what rank fear
That men will come prospecting with crowbars
Or slip in dogs at the mouth of our shorn hill.

The cold or fire; or to be sat out
By hunger; or as at Trehowlek
Where there were grave finds: a doll,
A photograph, the family loving cup.

At Pendeen something unspeakable
Must have happened to the woman of the house.
She appears in winter in a white dress
Biting a red rose.

Christmas

If his snowy manoeuvres
His chimneyings
Always seemed feasible
Why should not the big ship

After the seven seas
Sail our curdled river
Our stunk canal
And the unlit alley alley-o?

When the sky shrieked
And shapes were nosing through the water
And our big hospital
That could have blazed like a liner

Tried to hide, the galleon
Flew in like an owl
All sails breathing
Hoarsely like a baby

Behind the blackout
Hove to in our front room
And put off towards you
A coracle of oranges.

Hyacinths

The tortoise earth seems to have stopped dead.
Certainly the trees are dead, their limbs
Are broken, we can hear them clattering.
It must be about the midpoint. Last year
At this time you knelt for the hyacinths.

You brought them in like bread, in fired bowls,
From secret ovens of darkness. Three or four rooms
Soon had a column and a birth. Pictures show
The crib shining similarly
When Christ flowered from Mary the bulb.

The Kings stand warming their hands on the light.
Their gifts are nothing by comparison.
I suppose they feared that without some miracle,
Without the light and the bread of hyacinths,
The earth would never nudge forward out of the dark.

Mappa Mundi

1

This was a pleasant place.
This was a green hill outside the city.
Who would believe it now? Unthink
The blood if you can, the pocks and scabs,
The tendrils of wire. Imagine an apple tree
Where that thing stands embedded.

2

There is nowhere on earth now but
Some spoke will find us out
Some feeler from the impaled hill. On sunny days
That broken thing at the dead centre
Its freezing shadow comes round. At nights
Turning and turning like
The poor shepherd Cyclops for his bearings
It colours moonlight with a hurt eye.

3

Blood then, in a downpour.
For weather continued, the sun
Still drank what sea was available.
The indifferent wind herded his sagging clouds
That wept when they could not bear anymore.

4

Our nearest sea lies at the mercy of certain rivers.
The rivers themselves cannot avert themselves.
They begin blindly where, so we believe,
There is clean ice, snow and rare blue flowers.
They come on headlong and before they know it
We have them in our cities.

If they could die that would be better.
If they were lambs and we their abattoirs.
But they emerge like many of our children
Suddenly old, big-eyed,
Inclining to apathy. What was before
What they saw in our cities
They cannot at all remember. Day after day
They sink their trauma in the helpless sea.

5

The flat earth is felloed with death.
At every world's end, in some visited city,
Diminished steps go down into the river of death.
The salt river fills the throats of severed bridges.
Mors, the serpent, encircles the world.
His tail is in his mouth. He lives for ever.

6

Paradise lay in the river of death.
Before we slept we listened to the lapping water.
Our sands went steeply down, we bathed,
Rolling for joy like dolphins. Smiling,
We felt the dry salt on our faces;
Salt on our lips. She could halve
The mouth-watering apples exactly with her fingers.

We had four cardinal springs, they rose at the centre.
They rose from a love-knot continually undoing.

One day Charon arrived in a black boat,
One morning early, we were still sleeping.
Naked we were taken away from home.

7

The rivers of Paradise swam under the sea,
Unmixed with salt, death had no hold on them.
They surfaced miles apart, like fugitives
They calmed their breathing, they assumed
A local pace and appearance. Inland somewhere
Ordinary people
Receive driftwood from their broadcasting arms.

8

All rivers, even this, remain persuasive.
We have a house whose open windows listen.
At nights, my hand on your cold hand that rests
Upon your belly where our child curls,
We listen anxiously. Suppose we left,
Suppose we left this place and leaving below us
City, town, village and the interference
Of fence and throttling wire, suppose we found
The crack in the ice where one of the four emerges
Thrown, gasping, lying in the thin air
Like lambs that wait for strength from the sun to stand,
What could we do, holding that dangling thread?
Where could we go, knowing our need for breath?

Frightened at nights, hearing our city river,
We feel through our divining hands the pulse
Of the first four springs, we feel the kick
Of their departure diving, sweet through salt,
Their shouldering like smooth seals,
Their wriggling through the earth's rock like white hot quartz
Passing the creatures pressed
With starting eyes in carapaces
Whom fire and weight put out from the shape they had.

9

We shall not harm them now, they seem to pity us.
They have come out of a few last hiding-places.
They are solemn and curious, they have formed a ring.
Little by little they are coming forward, shy as birds.
We might have fed them. Or perhaps they are drawn
Against good manners, thinking it rude to stare, but as
Our children used to be drawn to pavement corpses
When deaths were singular. They are all true, all those
That we imagined; but many we never imagined.
They stare particularly at our little ones
Who cannot be frightened by anything we imagine,
Who are not alarmed by Blemyae and Sciapods,
By Dogheads, Cyclops, Elephant Men,
By some mouthless, feeding through a reed, others in a caul,
Some with the stumps of wings, some webbed, some joined, some
    swagged
With dewlaps, some diaphanous, some thin, with eyes.
Our children smile at them all. They are glad perhaps,
Our children, not to be unprecedented.

A Brightness to Cast Shadows (1980)

'Perfectly assured, beautifully crafted and rhythmically per-
suasive . . . an unevasive, but also subtle and tender treat-
ment of the timeless themes of poetry . . . an exciting and
stimulating first book' — SIMON RAE, *Quarto*

'His poems are both direct and subtle. His landscapes are
sensuously apprehended and arranged with a firm intellec-
tual control . . . a beautifully judged classicism' — JOHN MOLE,
Poetry Review

'Constantine celebrates erotic experience in verse sentences
of almost Jamesian intricacy and poise' — ROGER GARFITT,
Times Literary Supplement

'His stylistic mastery is married to beautiful and plangent
celebrations of the damned or the deceased. His art is as
socially conscious as it is harmonious. He shows a just and
stern concern about individual pain, suffering and insane
government policies. In places his shimmering and classical
illuminations fall with such intensity and conviction and his
denunciations with such power and delicacy that I have no
hesitation in placing him, thematically and formally, within
the great Dantesque tradition' — DAVID ANNWN, *Anglo-Welsh
Review*

Watching for Dolphins (1983)
ALICE HUNT BARTLETT PRIZE 1984

'David Constantine has a generous, self-aware sensuality
which he can express in a dazzling variety of tones on a
wide range of themes . . . His particular gift is for the re-
working of classical myths and Biblical narratives in such
a way that they are infused with ordinary, accessible emo-
tion and a sense of rich, humane acceptance' — FLEUR ADCOCK
and MARINA WARNER, *Alice Hunt Bartlett Prize commendation*

'Constantine's imagination moves gracefully within the classical precincts of the pure lyric, a Gravesian Muse poetry tempered with scholarship . . . intricate sensuality and an honesty of purpose that is impressive' – GEORGE SZIRTES, *The Litrerary Review*

'David Constantine's poems are brought back glittering from the Eastern Mediterranean and the hedges of Oxfordshire. They are stylishly written . . . cut from bolts of lyrical language. His obsession with the risen dead, with Lazarus and Jairus's daughter, shows him at his most original' – PETER PORTER, *Observer*

Davies (1985)

Davies was famous for a moment in 1911 when Home Secretary Winston Churchill raised his case in the House of Commons. But who was Davies? In this fictionalised account of a lifelong petty criminal, Constantine unravels the mystery of a shadowy loner caught in a vicious circle of self-perpetuating crime.

'*Davies* is a remarkable achievement, and not least for its bitter frugality of style . . . Constantine pieces Davies together from mist and myth, godly persecution and tolerance . . . The result is absorbing and disturbing' – CHRISTOPHER WORDSWORTH, *Guardian*

'The poet David Constantine speaks up for the socially edged-out . . . In *Davies*, Constantine's spare bare-knuckle prose makes marvellously present the harsh existence of his hero' – VALENTINE CUNNINGHAM, *Observer*

'Constantine's unabashed seriousness has marked him out as a very European writer – an impression confirmed by his first novel *Davies*, which, with its documentary neutrality of tone and muted outrage at injustice, recalls, for example, the Böll of *The Lost Honour of Katharina Blum* much more than any contemporary British novelist's work' – TIM DOOLEY, *Times Literary Supplement*

David Constantine was born in 1944 in Salford, Lancashire. He read Modern Languages at Wadham College, Oxford, and from 1969 to 1981 was a lecturer in German at Durham University. He is now Fellow in German at the Queen's College, Oxford. He is married with two children, and lives in Oxford.

His first book of poems, *A Brightness to Cast Shadows* (Bloodaxe Books, 1980), was widely acclaimed. His second collection, *Watching for Dolphins* (Bloodaxe Books, 1983), won the 1984 Alice Hunt Bartlett Prize, and his academic study, *Early Greek Travellers and the Hellenic Ideal* (Cambridge University Press, 1984), won the first Runciman Prize in 1985. His first novel, *Davies*, was published by Bloodaxe in 1985.

In 1988 his *Selected Poems* of the German poet Friedrich Hölderlin will appear from Bloodaxe, and his critical introduction to the poetry of Hölderlin from Oxford University Press.

He is now writing a stage adaptation of his novel *Davies* for Theatr Taliesin and the Made in Wales Stage Company.